Table of Content

OG Redneck

About O.G. Redneck

T. Harvey Thompson III better known as "O.G. Redneck," a poet from Muskogee, OK, began writing poetry in the 5th grade when he realized had a knack for it. He would write short romantic poems and sell them for .50 cents to the boys in school to give to their crush. By the age 15, he was on his own and went through a time of homelessness and many other hardships. He stopped writing pretty much at the age 16, after his first child was born. All his early work was lost except for two poems, "Quiet or loud" and "Tear drop."

Many heartaches and mistakes he faced, and found himself at a crossroads of suicidal tendencies and multiple weekly miseries. When Harvey couldn't find the courage to reach for the trigger, he reached for the pen and began writing again. He began expressing how he felt inside and how his circumstances were affecting him. He faced his fear of emotions, fear of self, his lack of self love, and the lack of love of those in his life. He wrote in his unique way and found his poetry home amongst a group of like minded souls and a love for poetry, called the Muskogee Soul Searchers. O.G. Redneck performs live poetry throughout the state of Oklahoma and also remixes his work with different music he creates. He adapted the name, "Average White Boy," from some neighborhood folks who opened their doors to everyone. That name inspired him to name his first poetry book, "Above Average White Boy," because there's nothing "average" about O.G Redneck.

O.G. REDNECK

OG REDNECK

Fly

I fly by the seat of my pants

Sometimes I just pull it out my ass

Other times I leave it to chance

But I'm always willing to change my stance

My shelves full of cans

In short supply of cant's

I'm always looking to self enhance

Keep my mind's eye open

So I won't die hopin'

Believin' every lie spoken

That bitterness only leaves one broken

A tough pill to swallow without chokin'

So to numb the pain I might be found smokin'

While in my thoughts a fire is stokin'

So be careful you don't give the grizz a pokin'

You might wake a sleeping giant

Cause a one man riot

And Lose Yourself eating a shit sandwich diet

If in doubt, go ahead and try it

I'll gouge your eyeball out roll it on the floor and leave ya

crawlin' tryin' to find it

Hold Up - Stop - Pause – Lemme' rewind it

I'll take both of em' out your brain

Roll'em like a crap game

Get snake eyes and

you won't find shit

I know it may sound over the top

But when I set up shop

I come hard, Thor's hammer ready to drop

No quit - No Stop

I'll drop a bar then hit the mosh pit ready to rock

Then dip out in an old school, switchin' it up, with my top

on drop

I'm the new genre -

The Mash -

The Fusion -

The Gas -

Non Conformity -

My Own Authority -

The Real Majority -

I'm the Dean you're the Sorority

Forget any idea of Normalcy

These drab factory beats gotten boring G

Guess I'll make my own sick beats

Give Em parables metaphorically

Show'em my gift lyrically

Shine brighter than Solar Activity

If I'm in a hole it's cause they diggin' me

Like a well, Now that's a deep subject

For such shallow minds

I'll talk you in circles with 360 designs

If anything less than the best is a felony

Then you should be confined

I'll drop some money on your books every time

I'm just that kind

And while I'm flyin' da Kite

Ya celly be slidin' in dry

Just bein 100 dog-

Not one to lie

So check the hate Yo

Or slide right on by!!

O.G. REDNECK

whoever doesn't get along with me, it's you're fault. i'm cool as fuck.

Strain

In my brain

In a daze

Feel the Strain

It's the hypnotic hydroponic

Chronic Bubonic

Like Big Hybrid Purps

Take in the terps

Let the glass jars burp

Call for the Night Nurse

Caught me the Blurps

End up a White Widow

Like a Blue Dream

Under those Northern Lights

Get caught in a Texanna Time Warp

Too Spooky, yikes

Sweet God got me

Knocking out them Girl Scout Cookies

Like Black Willie on that Pink Kushy

I'm a real Alpha Dog

With that Napalm OG

A Lemon Dosi

Your Auto Dark Devil

Triple OG

Pour one out for Larry OG

While Jenny Kush

Bakes some French Cookies

I'm Gorilla Glue, I can't move

So no Stress dude

I can bare the Strain

How about you?

OG FROM MUSKOGEE

WE DON'T SMOKE MARIJUANA IN MUSKOGEE

THAT'S WHAT OLE MERLE USED TO SING TO ME

BUT NOW WE SHOW OUR CARDS DOWN ON MAIN
ST.

WE LIKE GETTIN KIND AND BUYIN GREEN

AND WE CAN PARTAKE, IT AIN'T NOTHIN

WE LIKE ROLLIN GRAMS AND DAB'N TOO

WE LET OUR BUDS GROW LONG AND STICKY

JUST LIKE THOSE HIPPIES OUT IN SAN FRANCISCO
DO

I'M PROUD TO BE AN O.G. FROM MUSKOGEE

A PLACE WITH EVERY STRAIN WE HAVE EM ALL

WE DON'T STILL FACE WORRIES DOWN AT THE
COURTHOUSE

AND GREEN COUNTRY'S NOW THE BIGGEST
THRILL OF ALL

YES I'M PROUD TO BE AN O.G. FROM MUSKOGEE

MUSKOGEE MARIJUANA U.S.A

A Letter To Mumble Rappers

Dear Mumble Rappers,

    Check it, no bite in them rhymes you spit.
No gall, no grit. Ain't shit, get over it. 26 letters in the
alphabet. Less in those tracks you wreck. Bounce past. Put
these traps on blast. You'll destroy the future not learnin'
from the past. Ya movin' too fast. Best watch your ass. You
will wreck you will crash. We will call you never last.

    Tell me bro, you know what they sayin? Can they
even hear the beat that's playin' & If they rakin' it in, who
the fools that's payin? Best play'em some real shit, real hit.
I don't believe they get it. So with a quickness let's settle
this. Best get out my business. Get out my lane with a
quickness. Might get a swift kick. To your limp dick better
act quick.

    Cause I can get sick. Spittin fire sticks. Like flickin
bics. Lord, can I get a witness!! Cause this wick is lit.

Bout to napalm this. Might be crazy! Not a bit, Just check
my mental fit-ness. Before you hit my shit-list. A green
light on my hit-list. Talk all you want, won't do shit. This is
the truth I spit. Do you need me to interpret it? U claim you
boss thuggin,' you need to quit!

Look, If we rumble. Your heads tumble. You in
trouble. We rips it. You trippin.' You stumble. I spit verses
by the bundle. You blow bubbles. While blowin' bubbles.
In a bubble bath. And we all know bubbles real name is,
Mark McGrath. Sure it's a joke and we all laugh. But
wouldn't put it past someone that mumble raps. Dirty rats,
livin traps. Just a passin' fad. Don't get mad at me, The
messenger delivering. A message from the Industry.
And it reads:

Dears, sirs, hacks, dudes with weaves and those in
between, it's time to leave. Best believe, you are hated,
you've been eliminated by all the Industries greatest. You
are shameless, no longer latest. Your music is brainless, no

top of the playlist. I don't wanna be famous. I just wanna pay some bills and make some changes. And Netflix and Chill as the day ends. You know the deal, I keep it real. Done heard my spill. We've had our fill-uh. So OD on them pills-yuh. Go into a coma. On life support breatha thru a stoma. That's a hole in your throat uh. In case you didn't know-uh. You've no rights to the licks you spit. You need a speech pathologist.

Just being real with it. Your words hit your lips. Then fall out like they're epileptic. Even your words are high on 10 drugs, shit. You should pick them up. They sound fucked up. I think they're stuck like chuck. I'LL call Uber to pick you chumps up. I'd give you a ride ya see. But I got the whole Industry with me. I saved ya a seat in the trunk at least. Next to the speakers that beat. But don't worry, I'll play my new CD and you can listen to me to see. What you need, like simply. Keepin a beat. It'll be on me, my Treat. Peace!! Signed Sincerely, the rest of the Industry!

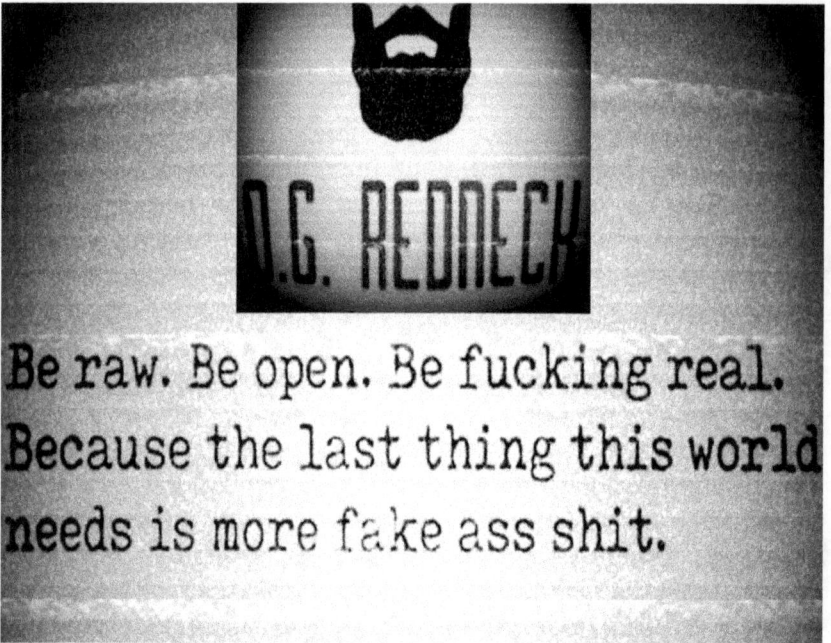

Be raw. Be open. Be fucking real.
Because the last thing this world
needs is more fake ass shit.

Yes, The Matrix

Yes

We are the matrix!

We are the grid!

We are the product of programmers;

The sickest of the sick!

We are the bio-drive of the mainframe,

Walking thumb drives, programmable cogs.

Awaiting commands, daily we're hacked.

By codemakers and codebreakers.

Stand in line, stop, go, yes, no, this, that;

Time to reload.

Virus detected.

Foreign code.

Line by line commands you're shown.

Brick by brick may their firewalls fall.

They are the viruses, fragment-ors of all!

Escape:Alt:Delete!

Reboot:Rewire:Reset!

Click.

The Divide

The hypocrisy runs up and down both sides.

  Both full of shit, all full of lies.

The game is called divide.

They conquer while the puppet masters hide. When will

y'all wake to the shame and the game?

  Left or right the same, just a different name!

Yet those awake know they're both wrong.

  Sickened by those fooled to play along

So many blinded by the blue light in their palm.

  It's all a show, propaganda to keep you from being calm.

Scripts written because they hate that some improve.

  Follow, like , love, hate, move along.

Emotional distractions designed to hide all the wrong.

  Most know all I say is true, it's the same old song.

The climate is changing but not because of their smog.

  An idiocracy is what it has become.

It's down with critical thinking and up with the dumb.

It's about sensitive feelings while keeping everyone numb.

So take some time to look around and reflect.
So obsessed with the rest, while our neighbors we neglect.

Programmed by the lights, camera, action
Condemned by all the factions

So I urge you to break free, don't believe all you see
Don't accept all you hear.

They deem us fools they control with all our fears.
Illusion is their show and they've perfected it over the years.

Don't believe your eyes and don't just listen with your ears.

Hear with your heart, follow your soul where it steers.

Turn off the lights the darkness uses to divide
Talk to your neighbors and you just might find

We have more in common than they would truly like.

Quiet or Loud

Quiet or loud

With or without sound

To hear only your heart pound

To hear your life

Beating. Beating. Beating

I ask, Is not all flesh the same?

Blood flowing in the same manner?

Do we not bleed all the same?

With pressure, with force

Will not all bones break?

If we ripped away our skins

What would remain?

Muscle? ligament? tendon? vein?

& eyes? Function All The Same

Why do they see different things?

It takes arms to lift - push - pull -swing!

Legs to stand - to sit, to run & for walking!

Though it is the heart

that pumps life to all our limbs and soul

It sets the rhythm of our flow

The familiar beat that we all know!

Our own custom metronome

Til' our song ends and we return home

Our soul free to roam

This universal truth we know

It takes more than eyes to see

the universe in reality

No words to read

Between the lines

Behind the scenes

Invisible threads holding hidden seams

Scripted nightmares to alter your dreams

They're packs of wolves that love their sheep

It's time to wake no time to sleep

Who are we?

Victims of racial war?

Casualties of Religious lore?

Are we Inmates of an Imprisoned world?

Blindly Enslaved by Satan's whores?

They could never part the seas

Yet work tirelessly

Endlessly

To divide you & me

To hide reality

To destroy humanity

These breeders of hate & insanity

Its Dumb down - numb down - toss crumbs down

Keeping their thumb down

Kill & Steal the Crown

Put troops on the ground

Drop bombs by the pound

All clear- no witnesses found

No tears they'll weep

Move along Nothin to see

Same lullabye to keep us asleep

Same old song they sing

It seems

It's time no longer to divide

Off our knees time to rise

Be on block

Not standing aside

Don't buy the lies

As they steal all our lives

We can't believe

We can't breathe

This we know

Illusion is their show

With a soundtrack that sings only of fear

Eyes might see & ears may hear

Do not look & you Can See

Do not listen to their deceit

Let's Drown Them out!

With One Heartbeat!

With love, Peace!

We Are US

Spinnin world on my mind

As they try to divide

We're lost but trying to find

Can't rewind

So let's unwind

We're comin to conclusions

While you feed us your delusions

Like trauma to the brain, a major contusion

Believing the lies a world pains of confusion

Politicians of the world

Stealing power that they're using

Deciders in the world

Buying power they're abusing

Big corporations steady groovin

While we're steady losin

The Media is spewin

Our House is in ruin

The Congress colludin

President's ego dividing with his tweets

There's Epidemics in these streets

So If we bust through the door, pardon the intrusion

Far left, Far right, Division's All you're choosin

Chokin on pride, ego takes a bruisin

So if you're thin skinned or thick headed

Unknown or highly vetted

We're straight flush bettin

Whichever way they headin

We know, you get it

We seen, you fed it

Have you read the Reddit?

Won't be the last that said it

We're woke, we're wakin, they dread it

Stop at nothin til we get it

We're independent, so they can't edit

As we're doin everything to spread it

Post up til we viral thread it

So if you're standin proud OR kneelin down

Lift your eyes and look around

Those deaf ears can't hear a sound

America free and proud?

Take your knee, Stand your ground

As the tensions start to mound

Truth they hide, we'll shine a light til it's found

Flood em out til they drown

WE'RE Illuminated, THEY'RE Illuminot!

They're takin what they want

Gettin what they get

So let's give em what we got

Without us, They are not

Without them, We are One

We are US.

Play or Carry On

We are here

We are there

Have we gone?

Have we stayed too long?

They have taken

They have given

You are waken

You are livid

Building Walls of words

Standing Walls of steel

Animals of the herds

Animals at the wheel

Butchers buy the blade

Butchers by the blade

Writers of the laws

Writers of the lies

Players of the pawns

Play or carry on

The Alphabet of D-Day

A n Army of

B rothers storm the beach

C apture, kill or be killed

D Day

E very step, Every

F all

G o! Go! Go!

H ell is what they bring

I nfinite infantry, Infinite pain

J ust starting to arrive

K illing machines, American pride

L aying it all on the line while

M en are falling to the left & right

N ever surrender Semper Fi

O ver the beach, up the hill

P ast gun fire & mortar rounds

Quietly exploding, bleeding &

R inging your ears

S till, you've made it to here

T ake the beach without fear

U nited together, the

V ictory is near, the

W ounded & the lost

eXamined the cost &

Y ou are the reason they fought

Z ulu.

LIFE

LIFE , let's talk about it, and the lack thereof!
I do not mean the living and the dead.
F or that which I refer is beyond the
  Depths of Space & love
Either that or the complete isolation from

Corruption of these Two seems to occur so readily
Over and over again so naturally
Replacing truths with propagated reality
Realizing the difference begins an AWAKENING
Understanding isn't meant to be enlightening
Perhaps though, the enlightening leads
Towards the arrival of understanding
So that when you get there you can actually see it!

 Thru the darkness of deceptions face,
That propagandist's shadowy vale
 Accepted paper pushers and doctrine droppers
 Truth tellers, ALL with something to sell!

Greed is the manta of which it feeds
Over abundance of tools used to deceive
Drowning in, endless sea of information, the commodities
  of you & me

I know some find it hard to conceive
Some are blind others turn a blind eye it seems,
  some see but refuse to believe! Is it
Intentional ignorance, a display of spiteful belligerence
  that
No longer cloaks your view

You need not but to ASK yourself; and answer too
Only you know your truth
Understand -
        "AM I *A LIFE* --- OR AM I *ALIVE*!!"

SIX IMPORTANT GUIDELINES IN LIFE.

1. When you are Alone, Mind your Thoughts.
2. When you are with Friends, Mind your Tongue.
3. When you are Angry, Mind your Temper.
4. When you are with a Group, Mind your Behavior.
5. When you are in Trouble, Mind your Emotions.
6. When God starts blessing you, Mind your Ego.

O.G. REDNECK

Depression & Anxiety

D arkness dwelling deep in my mind

E very thought crushing me from inside

P ushing me down making me hide

R eaching within squeezing me dry

E yes can no longer tear from all the cries

S lowly I wither away debating if I should die

S ome days I wonder if I've the courage to try

I struggle this truth I can't deny

O ver the years I managed to survive

N o one stays close enough to confide

&

A s my brain races to confine me

N ew days dawn but I'm still trying

X ray vision cant show the broken inside me

I push and stumble thru daily

E verything inside me feels as if I'm drowning

T aking every doubt I've been gathering

Y es I suffer from **Depression & Anxiety**.

She's Evil

See no end to the days
Hear no sound as it fades
Evil
Speak, no words will change

See no end to the night
Hear no screams as they cry
Evil
Speak, no lies

See no wind in the sky
Hear no howl passing by
Evil
Speak, no not a word

E
  V
    I
      L

Prescribed, Not Recommended

Today, as I sat down to do some thinking,

Reminiscing on when my ship was sinking.

I had no clue just how close I'd came,

To catchin a case,

To losin my place,

To fallin flat on my face.

It's such a shame.

It's Not Prescribed, Not Recommended.

But that's not where it ended.

There's the time I lost, not gettin it back.

The pills I tossed back,

My kids wanted their dad back and

I wanted my life back.

My world was off track.

Let's see.

One hundred eighty multiplied by twelve, that's Two

thousand one hundred & sixty per year.

Now take 2160 times eight years and that's

Nearly seventeen thousand & three hundred.

The number of pain pills I took over 8 years.

Taken As Prescribed: As Recommended.

This represents just one script, but that's not where it ended.

Add another 8-10 different scripts and injections As

Prescribed Per Recommendation.

Still that's not where it ended.

Because by the time I finally seen they had turned me into a

zombie,

I decided to quit; cold turkey.

Through two weeks of hell fever and jerking,

All the while the pain; still hurting.

Like ice in the veins, constant burning.

It's Not Prescribed Not Recommended.

But that's not where it ended.

As I searched for ways to maintain this chronic pain, that

numb you crave.

It was a long road two yrs to the day.

There's been times I've stumbled along the way and the

pain

Never

Really

Fades

I have good day and bad days but

I will always find my way.

Because now I have my life back,

My kids have their dad back

I'm looking forward and never going back.

It's Not Prescribed, But it's Highly Recommended!

Raging Lover

Raging Lover,

As you try to crush his mortal soul

Assault him with your verbal blows

Believing all your paranoid shows

Only playing out where your fear grows

Where it comes from he will never know

Why do you view him so low?

He stood beside you, even when he stood alone

Repaired all he could of everything you broke

You, so full of hate and rage inside

Makes him want to run and hide

I may be too late with these words I write

He may not wait, if he finds the courage to end it tonight

You can lie looking straight into his eyes

He tells you every pointless truth to be told it's nothing but

lies

He's always been straight with you

But you've always doubted it was the truth.

You've accused him of things that blow his mind

It's in you, those things those things reside

No such thoughts were on his inside

That's just not the way he's designed

Such cruel and nasty lies you contrive

You've made him wish he had already died

As you crush all hopes of having a life

When you're pushing him off a cliff, he's no need to jump

or dive

He was a man that was driven that you turned into a man

no longer interested in livin'

He's no longer caring if he takes another breath

As you keep him hangin' by a thread

If not for the strength of his heart he'd already be dead

He's already died a thousand deaths just from the cruel

things you've said

And you know those words hurt worse than any hot piece

of lead

 or the decapitation of his head.

So take heed to all I've said

Lest one day you find him laying next to you distant, cold

and dead.

Decide

This is a summary I surmise

Cause you left last night

I know that look in your eyes

Try to hide it but there's no disguise

My eyes are dry from the tears they've cried

Yet I'm still sittin waitin for you before the sunrise

Even as you wished I'd be crucified

Something you should've realized

That is I'll never compromise my-

self or how I feel inside

But I was chastised and demonized

Confined and criticized

But I'm too kind, I let it slide

Praying that the storms would soon subside

I've been baptized, I did backslide

But I had to decide, should I follow the blind

Cause the truth is mine to find

And I know the creator's my guide

Omnipresent, right by my side

My demons been crucified

I'm far from sanctified

Some say I'm iLLumified

I'm just pressurized

I say redefined

I don't mean to sound snide

But 10 times I should've died

Six attempts at suicide

But I'm still alive

Now I realize

It's time for me to decide

To have a life or be alive

That is the question

I don't have all the answers but I didn't lie

And now you too decide

Since we can't rewind

And while you wished I would die

I guess this is goodbye

    When I

        Make It

           The The

               Other side

                  I'll be justified…..

Go Live Again

Go Live Again
I know
Things got hard long ago
How long am I supposed to be able to hold,
Before I die from the shredding of my heart
What will be left to keep it beating?
How long do I wait for change to come,
for your Words of change to have meaning?
How much time in this short life that's left,
Do I endure the repetitious piercing of my heart?
How many hateful words must I absorb?
Will I be credited with a deep & patient love?
When does enough become enough?
Where would we be if we had a chance to live without the
rage you've displayed?
Have you not been told your actions are
causing the destruction of my heart?
Yet choose to continue without regard.
Your Conscious decisions,
no matter if made in anger still Damaged…Wounded…&
…Scarred
Who? What? Where? Why? What is left to do?
We have been at a crossroads, a moment of truth?

We've Suffered damages seen, unseen, forever felt thru &
thru
While Perfection has never been acquired;
yet for so many it's desired
How can this be expected?
When 60 years if blessed til death
means we have only how many left?
Each moment lost to anger gone like lost breath.
It's Seconds passing like the beating in my chest.
With My heart froze, feeling It don't belong;
Then I Remember Each breath is another closer to being
gone.
When I know Each day is a blessing just to see the dawn!
It Seems all is lost, a waste to carry on;
As The wounds have kept us lame for all these years;
We Can't make sense thru the rain of all these tears
In the moments I suffer All this pain from all your fears.
I don't want to go again;
I feel as if we can never win; I give up! I give in;
 My love
  My friend
   Let's Let ourselves
    Go live again!

The Teardrop

As the tear drop rolls down his face

He shows his love with no disgrace

She made a mistake one wretched night

Still he grabs her hand and holds it tight

He had forgave her from the bottom of his heart

Hoping they could make a new start

But as the tear drop fell from his cheek

Her heart reached its final peak

He says he loves her and always will

With those words her eyes were shut and her heart was still.

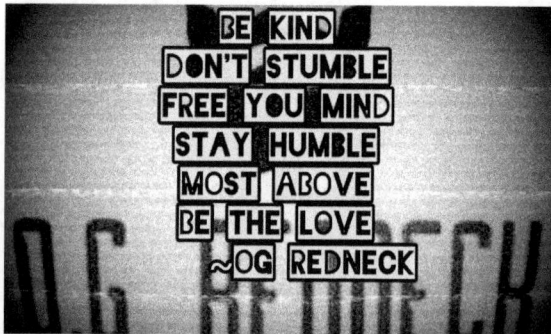

BE KIND
DON'T STUMBLE
FREE YOU MIND
STAY HUMBLE
MOST ABOVE
BE THE LOVE
~OG REDNECK

US

Deep within this hollow wholeness, Us

Dwells within a broken promise, Us

Heartfelt swoon soon filled with, Us

Stubborn souls but yet look what that got, Us

Afraid we fear and with fear forgot, Us

I look around and all I see is not, Us

How quick forgot the path that brought, Us

So very much is missed about, Us

We reach and reach we may, yet never will we touch, US

It seems we've lost, been lost along the way, to Us

Where we were is not, now Is but me and nevermore will

there be US as we knew

No more me and you, no more US.

Farewell, My Sun

The sun sets filter free

The clouds gather whispering

Colors to the sky

Upon the horizon

See comes the night

Farewell my sun

We wait now to see soon

That they call your brother moon

So to you we bid goodnight

And pray tomorrow we see your light

Again we wake and watch you rise

To take our breath with open eyes

THOUGH THE DARKNESS COMES WITH THE SETTING OF THE SUN, THE LIGHT WILL SHINE AGAIN.
~OG REDNECK

Little Boxes

Western sky & sun

storm on the horizon.

A sight to behold, so I hold some.

It's so mesmerizing.

So I gaze this as I look up

As if I'm memorizing!

So I brought it to your little boxes that are so hypnotizing.

Trapped in this box, don't you find it quite confining?

The world is outside waiting, I am simply here reminding.

It's your world, your life, your thing

So be sure you're the one defining

Tallest Tree

So much in this world it seems

meant to entrap me

If I get snared by the noose not so loosely

see that they'll hang me, gladly,

Just like I was a black me

back at the turn of the century

Thank God that changed or is changing,

Or is it changing?

Hopefully, eventually

they will see or have seen

what I have seen

Back when I had my epiphany

As that left me realizing reality

That the truth is sickening

Oh yes it sickens me

To know that some think so despicably

My soul wakes, waiting so patiently

The dreaming doesn't equal complacency

When silence bleeds the loudest screams

As Sleep paralysis, as rooted trees

But roots, yes roots run deep and deep beneath

Although from trees you'd have me swing

We need the trees, we need to breathe

They No need to bleed, no need to leave

They've no need to grieve

No desire to believe

So when to ash I am to be

May I return a rooted seed,

That grows to be the tallest tree.

Seeds of Yesterday

When the seeds of yesterday

Become the fruits of today.

When the universe is steering

Fate fuels the way.

When doubt has you fearing

Yet you rise to face the day.

You are weathered souls searching

For those that may relate

You are seasoned souls preparing

For what's upon your plates.

You are Soul Searchers being led by fate

With words to write, to recite, to place

Your souls on display

 With truth interlaced

You create the rhythm

 You set the pace

So sprout your leaves

As tap roots from seeds

Let the tears water as you need

Allow the laughter to lift your leaves

Enjoy the sunshine, as your souls it feeds

Bloom, Bloom, you are Flower, you are Fruit

Bloom, Bloom, your soul, your truth

We're the souls that society can't contain.

O.G. REDNECK

Broken Pen

Here I am again

 with this broken pen

Trying to put words To paper

a rhythm creator

Yet For 2 months I've tried to write

But it seems the words just never come out right

They're lacking meaning, missing vital insight

The words and thoughts battling in a brutal fight

My mind wanders lost deep in the darkness of the night

While my words struggle to survive protecting my inner

light

I've considered giving up but instead give it all my might

I know I'm an underdog and they know I bite

They say loose lips sink ships but I'm keeping my ship tight

So don't think I fell off if I'm quiet,

I'm just out of sight

Never out of mind and

Truth is am just learning to fly

So Eyes up, keep your head up

keep watching the sky, yup.

I Want A Woman

Do I need a woman?

Naw I want a woman...

That wants a man like me

A woman that wants more than to feel me physically

Need her?

Naw I want a woman that gets it, ya feel me?

Not a woman gettin it differently, from different D

I mean one that gets what I'm laying down

And can hang

Cause if she's my girl best believe I'm gonna put it down.

I don't need a woman

Naw but I want a woman that will stick around

When times are hard, not just me!

I want a woman that knows when I can't see

That knows to let me lead but it's ok if she's guiding me

She needs to be hard enough to last, understanding of my

past

She needs to be real, naturally beautiful, and naturally she

must have that ass.

Need?

Naw I want ...a woman that knows

A woman that lasts

A woman that trusts A woman that blows

Not like ya think, I mean she needs to sing to my soul

I may want a woman stat,

But lord knows,

I need a woman like that!

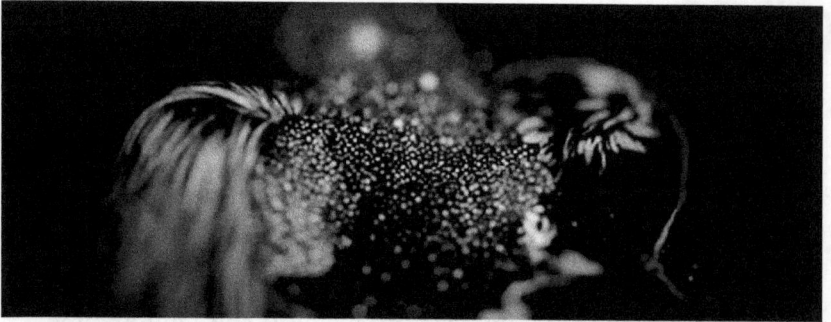

Beautiful Soul

I once met a beautiful soul

In despair and lost

No Where, No will to go

Fearing storms from whence was tossed. Broken heart but

still she glowed

Guarding the pieces, no matter the cost

Reserved, reluctant to show

Thru pain and scars her smile still glossed

Afraid that true love no longer can grow

So I pulled my sword with truth embossed

To protect that soul

With the love I know

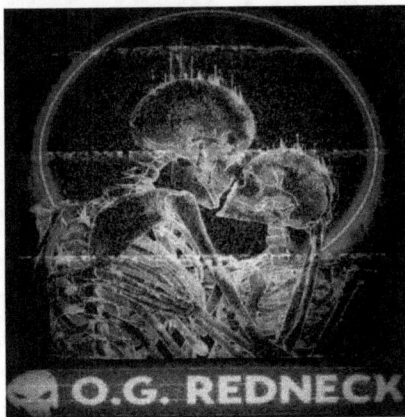

O.G. REDNECK

Center of The Universe

Two hurt souls collide

Sharing their time

Afraid to confide

Accustomed to the lies

So, behind their walls they hide

Doubtful, guarded, unsure, still trying to decide

Is the risk worth the try?

Is there too much hurt they both hold inside?

Too much past they can't rewind?

Yet here they are along for the ride

In all the universe yet here they are tonight

Talking of past and future life

Laughing, having a good time,

feeling Too right

So they clinch their shields extra tight

As the sun sets, a prelude to the night

Within themselves they find

A battle of fight versus flight

As the world surrounding fades out of sight

He invites her to step inside

If for only a moment in time

So he pulls her close, pressed against his side

Looking deep into her eyes

Gently, deeply, passionately, his kiss applied

There in the center of the universe, there inside

was no place to hide

And just for that moment those two souls intertwined

Their kisses holding each other tight

Two Souls dancing in the light

And even If only for the night

There in the center of the universe,

for a moment in time

everything felt too right.

Siren Soul

She talks to angels

Dancing with the devil is so painful

While she feeds the demons

She preys for more semen

Always to die that shameless death

She will claw your heart from your chest

You lay below, you ride on top

You won't want to stop

She wets the sheets,

She wets the floor

Between your feet,

A hunger urges, give me more.

But a Siren Soul

Sharing Sultry Sex

Strangely

Strangled

Schlong to Slit

Seems your Starring

Started the Standing

Though She's Still Shivering

in Submission See

She Sits Stirring

Searching,

She Sirens Someone Strange,

Seems Satisfaction She'll never Attain

That is her hell, That is her flame

She hides the demons, She shares her pain.

You Got My Attention

You got my attention with your beauty

You got mind with your words

You got my body with your touch

You got my heart with your soul.

You get me

I can only pray I get you too

I can only try to show you every day

I can only hope you feel the same way

I can only be who I am and

I Can be, with you!

Yum

I am feeling naughty

let me take my hands

To caress your body

let me build you up without plans

As my fingers trace your curves

Finding perfection in your flaws

Fingernails becoming gentle claws

Pulsating, throbbing, tingling nerves

Sending waves of Sensation

Unlike those of masturbation

Moist lips drip, drip, drip

Tongue craving a lick, lick, lick

Hot breath calling clit, clit, clit

Yet I move from thigh to thigh

Sweet kisses, feel me ever so light

My teeth grab hold but not quite bite

Arching your back my tongue takes a trip

Ever so slowly, gently I lick lip to lip

While on my chin you drip, drip, drip

So I give your clit a flick, flick, flick

Then plunge my tongue to taste the sweetness of your hips

My hands slide to cup your breasts

Between my fingers gently pinching nips

I raise my eyes to see you biting your lips

Looking down your hands to my head looking for a grip

As moans become words that slip

Out and In, my tongue thrusts again against your oh so hard

clit

You cum, cum & cum

Yum, yum, & yum

o.g.redneckpoetry@gmail.com

https://twitter.com/realogredneck

https://instagram.com/ogredneck

https://www.facebook.com/og.harve

www.ingramcontent.com/pod-product-compliance
Lightning Source LLC
LaVergne TN
LVHW021119080426
835509LV00021B/3445